LEARNING TO LOVE MYSELF AFTER BREAKUP

A Step-by-Step Guide on How to Recover and get Over a Heartbreak, Let Go of Your Ex, Find Your Self-Worth, and Heal Your Broken Heart

KATY ROBIN

Copyright © 2024 by Katy Robin

All rights reserved. No part of this book may be reproduced or transmitted in any form or by any means, electronic or mechanical, including photocopying, recording, or by any information storage and retrieval system, without permission in writing from the publisher.

The information provided in this book is designed to provide helpful information on the subjects discussed. The author and publisher disclaim any liability or loss in connection with the use or misuse of this information. It is recommended that readers consult with appropriate professionals before taking any actions based on the information in this book.

TABLE OF CONTENTS

CHAPTER 1 9

    THE AFTERMATH 9

        Coping with Grief: Understanding the Kübler-Ross Model 10

        Finding Comfort in the Early Stages of Grief 18

        Making Peace with Your Grief 22

        Heartbeats of Hope 30

CHAPTER 2 31

    LETTING GO - DETACHING FROM YOUR EX 31

        The Key to Letting Go 32

        The Detachment Protocols 33

        Letting Go of the Myth of Validation and Closure . 38

        Strategies for Maintaining Zero Contact after a Breakup 45

        I Deserve Better 47

CHAPTER 3 49

    PLAYING THE EX GAMES 49

        Establishing Boundaries 51

Overcoming Destructive Habits 58

Preserving Your Mental Well-being 68

Learning to Take Care of Yourself 72

Unshackled 78

CHAPTER 4 79

MOVING ON 79

Self-Sabotage... No More 80

What to Avoid when Starting Afresh 85

Conclusion 88

I Am Going to Heal 90

INTRODUCTION

If you've picked up this book, chances are you're currently navigating the aftermath of a recent heartache. It's probable that whatever occurred, it left a lasting sting. Maybe your relationship unraveled in a heated argument, or perhaps it quietly dissipated until one day, after many years, you realized the love was gone. It could be that a hurtful comment from your partner shattered your confidence. Alternatively, you may have parted ways amicably, promising to stay friends no matter what.

Now, you're likely finding yourself alone. Depending on the timeline, you might still be stuck in a routine, absentmindedly memorizing TV schedules. Or perhaps you're out and about, going through the motions of daily life, pretending everything is fine. You probably have friends who've weathered their own heartbreaks, recalling how they went from sadness to socializing. You might wonder if they were truly coping or merely putting on a brave face. Maybe you're even considering diving into another relationship, yet your thoughts keep drifting back to your ex.

Regardless of your circumstances, heartbreak is undeniably painful. Coping with the sudden absence of someone significant is challenging, and even those who appear to have moved past the despair still experience moments of longing for what once was. During vulnerable moments, you might question whether you'll ever fully recover from this heartache and move forward with your life.

Enter this book. It offers guidance on navigating your breakup and healing from the ensuing heartache, helping you rediscover yourself with renewed optimism and aspirations.

This book is for everyone, regardless of their relationship type or sexual orientation, be it heterosexual, homosexual, or bisexual, regardless of gender. Whether you're facing the end of a seven-year marriage, finding yourself single in your later years, or mourning the conclusion of a passionate college romance, this book is tailored to you. You might be skeptical about whether it can offer relevant advice, but rest assured, it's designed for individuals from all walks of life. Despite the perceived differences in relationships, humans share similar emotional responses and stages. Loss is a universal experience, as is the journey of recovery. No matter where you were in your relationship or what form it took, there's something within these pages for you.

Believe it or not, we're all in this together.

Heal My Soul

Let the warmth of love shine bright

Into the depths of my darkest night

Heal my soul, restore my heart

Let me find my way, a brand new start

Let go of the pain, let go of the fear

And fill me with hope, year after year

Mend the cracks, repair the tears

And let my spirit soar, free from all fears

Heal my soul, revive my mind

Let me find my strength, leave the past behind

Let love and light, guide me on my way

And lead me to a brighter, brand new day.

CHAPTER 1

THE AFTERMATH

COPING WITH GRIEF: UNDERSTANDING THE KÜBLER-ROSS MODEL

When you experience a significant loss, like a breakup, it's natural to feel a profound sense of grief, similar to what people feel when someone close to them passes away. This reaction is completely normal and expected. According to recent psychological research, individuals facing terminal illness or enduring catastrophic losses typically go through five stages of grief. These stages were first outlined by psychiatrist Elisabeth Kübler-Ross in 1969 and are collectively known as the Kübler-Ross model. It's important to note that you don't have to be facing death or be close to someone who is dying to go through these stages—experiencing heartbreak is loss enough.

Stage #1: DENIAL

Denial marks the initial stage of the Kübler-Ross model. In this stage, you resist accepting that the relationship has ended. Denial becomes easier if your ex hasn't been direct about breaking up with you. For example, if she expresses a desire to date other people, you might convince yourself that it's just a temporary change and she'll come back to you eventually. Similarly, if he wants to take a step back in the relationship, you might convince yourself that he just needs some space. However, some individuals remain in denial even when their exes are clearly expressing their intentions to end the relationship.

Denial presents itself in three main forms. The first is simple denial, where you outright refuse to acknowledge that the breakup has occurred. For instance, you might say, "He didn't break up with me. He simply mentioned he's considering dating other people." While this form of denial is straightforward, it's challenging to convince yourself that something hasn't happened when it clearly has. Simple denial is often observed in response to severe traumas, like rape or terminal illness.

Another form of denial is minimization, where you acknowledge that something has happened but downplay its significance. For example, you might think, "She mentioned breaking up, but she didn't mean it. She's just emphasizing the importance of punctuality."

The third form of denial is projection. Here, you accept the facts and their seriousness but deflect responsibility onto someone else—typically, your ex. While this form of denial is rarely used to deny the breakup itself, it may come into play when assigning blame for the breakup.

However, denial eventually comes to an end. It has to because continuing to deny reality becomes increasingly challenging. While you might be able to live in denial about certain things, like failing a test or being overweight, denying a breakup becomes unsustainable when your ex begins dating other people. At that point, you're forced to confront reality, either on your own or through a confrontation. Unfortunately, facing the truth means delving into the subsequent stages, which often involve negative emotions.

Stage #2: ANGER

Moving on to the next stage of the Kübler-Ross model: anger. When a relationship ends, the anger that surfaces is often akin to feeling unfairly treated or harmed by someone else. Individuals in this stage constantly question why they're experiencing this loss and why others don't seem as affected. This can lead to overwhelming feelings of anger and envy, projecting these emotions onto others rather than directing them inward or toward their ex-partner.

Anger can manifest in two primary ways: aggressively or passively. Aggressive anger involves behaviors you'd expect, such as verbal or physical threats, bullying, or even destructive tendencies like breaking things or harming others. People expressing aggressive anger may also exhibit selfish behaviors or display manic energy, engaging in excessive spending or intense physical activities.

On the other hand, passive anger, also known as passive aggression, is not expressed as directly. It may involve performing self-sacrificing acts while secretly resenting others for not appreciating them fully. Individuals might criticize themselves publicly, apologize excessively, and invite criticism from others. They may also avoid conflict, back away from challenges, or develop a fear of confrontation.

Both forms of anger, whether expressed aggressively or passively, are common responses to the pain of a breakup.

In more subtle ways, passive anger can manifest as obsessive behavior, where individuals strive for perfection in everything they do, even in activities that are best approached with moderation, like dieting or exercising. Passive anger can also lead to ineffectiveness, where individuals set themselves up for failure by ignoring important issues while focusing on trivial ones, relying on unreliable people, or experiencing frequent accidents. In its extreme form, passive anger can become dispassionate, causing individuals to withdraw from emotional connections with others and instead focus on objects or intellectual pursuits. When forced to interact with others, emotionally dispassionate individuals may come across as insincere, lacking empathy, and preferring to avoid taking responsibility for problems.

Passive anger can be just as damaging as aggressive anger, often manifesting in psychological manipulation. This manipulation might involve provoking others to behave aggressively while pretending to be innocent, subtly insulting them, spreading gossip, or even engaging in theft and deceit.

After reading about these expressions of anger, you might feel like someone who's angry is a ticking time bomb ready to explode onto the world. However, it's important to remember that feeling angry is a natural human emotion, especially during a breakup. Additionally, only a minority of people resort to such extreme expressions of anger, whether aggressive or passive.

During a breakup, the individual who was dumped may feel intense anger toward their ex-partner, as well as toward their ex's family and friends. This anger might even extend to their own loved ones. At this stage, the person experiencing anger may lash out at those offering help or comfort, saying things they later regret once they've had time to calm down.

Stage #3: BARGAINING

Welcome to the next stage of grieving: bargaining. This stage involves the belief that you can somehow postpone or even change the outcome of the breakup—if only you could identify that one thing that would make your ex change their mind. In this stage, as anger begins to fade, you find yourself contemplating what actions you could take to win back your ex's affection.

In traditional grief stages, bargaining often involves pleading with a higher power or fate itself to delay an inevitable event. Similarly, in the context of a breakup, bargaining represents a psychological step forward, indicating acceptance that the relationship is ending, even if you're attempting to stall the breakup.

Bargaining with another person differs from bargaining with death. In a relationship, you might believe that by saying or doing the right thing, you can persuade your ex to reconsider. Unlike death, your ex is capable of changing their mind, especially if they're experiencing their own feelings of remorse. However, you must realize that no single change on your part will magically repair the relationship. At best, it might delay the breakup, but it won't prevent it indefinitely.

Stage #4: DEPRESSION

After the battles have been fought and the attempts at bargaining have been made, depression begins to take hold. This stage involves the painful processing of grief, and it's not a pleasant experience. During periods of depression, feelings of hopelessness, sadness, and helplessness blend together, often leading the person to withdraw and become introspective. They may spend hours crying and mourning the loss of the relationship.

Those grappling with depression often lack the motivation to do anything. It's common to envision someone who's just experienced a breakup as sitting on the couch, indulging in ice cream or video games while watching TV for days on end.

The depth of depression following a breakup varies based on factors like the length and intensity of the relationship, as well as the amount of time spent together. Fortunately, this stage is temporary. Psychologists refer to it as situational or slight depression, and it typically resolves with time, rest, and support from loved ones. However, in some cases, severe or clinical depression may develop, necessitating professional psychiatric intervention. While not everyone who goes through a breakup will experience severe depression, it can be a significant risk factor, especially for vulnerable individuals.

Stage #5: ACCEPTANCE

The final stage of grieving is acceptance, marking the point where the individual acknowledges the loss and finds peace with it. They realize that although the pain of the loss will always be a part of their story, it won't define them.

In the acceptance stage, the person begins to re-engage with life. In terms of relationships, this may involve starting to date again or at least being open to the idea. They also take on responsibilities and tackle daily tasks that they may have neglected during earlier stages of grief. This stage is the most positive because it indicates readiness to move forward with life.

It's important to distinguish acceptance from resignation, which involves submitting to the loss while harboring negative emotions. While acceptance involves understanding and peace with the loss, resignation is marked by a sense of powerlessness and frustration. Although someone who's resigned may appear calm on the surface and continue with their routine, over time, it becomes evident that they lack the same zest for life and may be more pessimistic than before the loss.

Acceptance means facing reality as it is, while resignation involves giving up and succumbing to negativity.

FINDING COMFORT IN THE EARLY STAGES OF GRIEF

Breaking up with someone you cared about is really tough, whether you've been together for a year or for ages. Even if you were the one who ended things, it still hurts. You're not just saying goodbye to your ex, but also to the future you had imagined together.

The first few weeks and months after the breakup are often the hardest. You feel sad all the time and start doubting yourself and everything around you. Most people I talked to went through at least some of these feelings:

• Feeling shocked and unable to believe what's happened.

• Wondering if you'll ever be happy again or trust someone new.

• Feeling really down and finding it hard to cope.

• Feeling anxious, with shaky hands and a racing heart.

• Knowing deep down it's over, but hoping things will go back to how they were.

• Finding it hard to control your feelings, like crying all the time or getting mad easily.

• Feeling embarrassed that your relationship ended, and too ashamed to talk about it.

• Constantly trying to reach out to your ex, even though you know it's not helping.

• If you're getting a divorce, feeling totally overwhelmed by everything.

• Can't stop thinking about what went wrong, replaying it over and over in your head.

- Worrying about how your kids are handling things and feeling guilty.

- Blaming yourself and wishing you'd done things differently.

- Feeling really angry, like you're about to explode.

- Worried about money if your ex helped out financially.

- Feeling completely betrayed and shaken if the breakup was because of cheating.

- Feeling like time's running out and you'll never find happiness again.

- Not being able to eat or sleep properly.

- Feeling sorry for yourself and like nothing ever goes right.

- Feeling totally lost and not able to get anything done.

- Either making loads of plans to keep busy or just staying home and feeling lonely.

Maybe some of these feelings hit close to home for you. You might even relate to all of them. Each one represents a common reaction to a breakup. The first step toward healing is acknowledging that what you're feeling is totally normal.

Let me start by expressing my deepest sympathy for the pain you're going through. Breaking up is incredibly tough. How could anyone be prepared for this level of heartache? It can feel overwhelming and downright scary. I've been there, and so have countless others.

Now, you're knee-deep in the initial stages of grief after the breakup. Every day feels like an emotional rollercoaster ride—unfamiliar territory for most people. Many describe feeling like they're losing their minds as their mood swings wildly from one extreme to another. You're entering a whole new world, filled with thoughts and feelings you've never experienced before.

It's crucial to validate your feelings during this time. Recognizing that your emotions are valid helps ease some of the pain you're going through. Unfortunately, your ex often can't provide the validation you need, which can be really upsetting. You might try all sorts of ways to make them understand, but it rarely works out. Even well-meaning friends and family might not grasp the full extent of what you're going through, which can feel isolating. If you haven't found a way to validate your feelings on your own, it's important to start now. You can use this book and my words to help you through the healing process.

Remember, it's okay to feel whatever you're feeling. You have every right to feel miserable, and it's crucial to accept your grief. Validating your own feelings and allowing yourself to experience them fully is a crucial part of moving forward and healing.

MAKING PEACE WITH YOUR GRIEF

Surviving the initial aftermath of a breakup requires coming to terms with your sadness and recognizing that it won't fade away overnight. I get it—it goes against our instincts to embrace patience and gradual healing. Most of us, myself included, prefer to hit fast-forward and escape the pain as quickly as possible. But resisting your current emotions won't help; in fact, it might make things worse. It's crucial to cultivate patience and understand that healing takes time—there are no quick fixes.

It's common for people in the early stages of a breakup to ask, "When will I start feeling better?" or "Why am I still feeling this way?" It's completely normal to dislike suffering, but breakup pain serves a purpose—it's a necessary step toward healing, growth, and transformation.

Think of suffering in a spiritual sense. According to ancient Buddhist teachings, suffering diminishes as we progress on a path of self-improvement and enlightenment. As you embark on your journey, you'll come to see the wisdom in this approach.

Although the heartache may seem overwhelming now, trust me, with time and effort, you will bounce back. We'll navigate through this challenging period together, finding healthy ways to cope with your pain. We'll untangle your emotions, understand why the relationship ended, and equip you with valuable tools to move forward. While it may feel impossible today, it's highly likely that you'll emerge from this experience as your best self—healthier and happier than you ever thought possible.

Coping with Anger Positively

When you've lost something dear to you, feeling angry is completely natural. But it's crucial not to act on that anger in destructive ways. Repressing your anger isn't healthy either—it tends to seep out in other ways, making you resentful and irritable. You might find yourself snapping at people or delivering subtle insults without even realizing it.

To deal with your anger, the first step is to acknowledge it. Own up to your feelings—it's not your proudest moment, but it's necessary. Once you recognize your anger, you can start to manage it. Understand who or what you're really angry at—it's not the slow driver in front of you or the noisy kids in the park.

When confronting your anger, you might feel overwhelmed. But there are positive ways to channel that energy:

- Tear up any letters or messages from your ex—it's surprisingly satisfying.

- Get a punching bag or use a pillow to release pent-up frustration.

- Exercise at the gym or go for a swim to turn that energy into something positive.

- Talk to a supportive friend about how you're feeling.

- Blast some music and let out your emotions through song.

- Try meditation to calm your mind and soothe your anger with deep breaths.

By confronting and channeling your anger in healthy ways, you can begin to navigate through this challenging time with greater ease.

Dealing with Depression

As you confront and manage your anger, you may find yourself facing sadness on the other side. Sadness often follows anger, and experiencing depression after a breakup is entirely normal. When your feelings of love are rejected, it's natural to feel down. You might feel constantly tired, have trouble concentrating, or lack motivation to do anything. These are all signs of depression, which can drain your energy and leave you feeling listless.

During these periods of depression, it's essential to find ways to lessen your pain. Writing down your thoughts in a journal can help you organize your feelings and understand them better. Talking with friends can also provide comfort and support.

Focusing on positive thoughts can be beneficial when coping with depression. Reflect on positive moments from your day or week, no matter how small they may seem. Remind yourself of what you've accomplished, even if it's just getting through the day despite feeling

25

depressed. Listening to uplifting music or engaging in activities you enjoy can also lift your spirits.

However, if you find yourself experiencing deep depression or suicidal thoughts, it's crucial to seek help immediately. Deep depression is characterized by an inability to function and a lack of hope for things to improve. If you're unsure whether you're experiencing deep depression, a simple test is to ask yourself if you have hope for things to get better. If you feel hopeless, it's essential to reach out to a therapist or seek help from a trusted friend or family member.

Seeking help for mental health issues is not a sign of weakness; it's a smart and courageous decision. Remember, admitting you have a problem and facing reality takes strength, and getting help when you need it is a brave step towards healing. Don't hesitate to seek professional help if you're struggling with depression or suicidal thoughts.

Your Anxiety and Guilt

Anxiety and guilt often accompany the aftermath of a breakup, and both can be quite distressing. Anxiety can manifest as a feeling of restlessness or escalate into a state of heightened alertness, where even the slightest movement or noise can feel overwhelming. Physical symptoms like shaking hands and a racing heart are common, and severe anxiety may disrupt sleep and appetite. While medication can help, practicing relaxation techniques can also be beneficial.

Creating a designated relaxation space in your home, complete with calming elements like candles, soothing music, and comfortable lighting, can provide a sanctuary for moments of anxiety. By visualizing yourself in a peaceful setting and focusing on deep breathing, you can gradually ease your mind and body into a state of relaxation.

Guilt, on the other hand, is a complex emotion that often arises after a breakup. Both parties may feel responsible for the relationship's end, whether due to perceived shortcomings or unresolved issues. It's natural to reflect on past actions and wonder if things could have been different, but dwelling on guilt can hinder your ability to move forward.

I want you to know that you cannot change the past or control the outcome of the breakup solely through apologies or self-blame. While acknowledging mistakes is important for personal growth, dwelling excessively on guilt is counterproductive. Instead, focus on learning from past experiences and applying those lessons to future relationships.

Consider journaling about your feelings of guilt and reflecting on how you can use those lessons to improve yourself in the future. If you feel compelled to apologize to your ex, consider writing a letter expressing your thoughts and feelings, but refrain from sending it until you've had time to process your emotions and move on.

Ultimately, taking responsibility for your actions and using them as opportunities for growth can be empowering.

Acceptance and Moving On

Reaching the acceptance stage after a breakup is a significant milestone, marking a shift towards inner peace and emotional stability. You may not even realize you've entered this stage until you notice moments of tranquility amidst the turbulence of emotions. Gradually, these moments of peace become more frequent, while feelings of depression and anger diminish.

Acceptance brings a newfound clarity about life's purpose and meaning. While there may not be a single right answer, you find an understanding that resonates with you. This clarity prompts a spiritual rejuvenation, prompting you to reevaluate your life and make significant changes based on your newfound perspective. You may pursue long-held dreams, explore new interests, or embrace opportunities for personal growth.

Embrace this phase with gratitude, acknowledging the strength and resilience you've gained through the breakup experience. Consider the goals you aspire to achieve and utilize the courage and wisdom you've acquired to pursue them wholeheartedly.

As you navigate this journey of acceptance and self-discovery, you may encounter challenges such as encountering your ex or finding new sources of joy without them. These are common hurdles, but with patience and resilience, you'll find your way forward. The answers to these questions and more are within reach, guiding you towards a future filled with possibility and fulfillment.

HEARTBEATS OF HOPE

In the silence, listen deep

To the rhythm that your heart does keep

A beat of hope, a pulse of grace

A reminder that a new dawn embraces

Your soul's resilience, like a drum

Beats strong and steady, never numb

To the pain, to the fear, to the night

It whispers "hold on, a new light"

In every darkness, a spark remains

A glimmer of promise, a heart that sustains

The fire of hope, a flame that burns bright

Guiding you forward, through the darkest night

So hold on tight, to the heartbeats of hope

And let them carry you, to a brand new scope

Of possibilities, of dreams yet to come

And a future bright, where love has won.

CHAPTER 2

LETTING GO – DETACHING FROM YOUR EX

THE KEY TO LETTING GO

My first love broke my heart into tiny pieces. It hurt a lot. I felt like I couldn't live without him. It was like losing a part of myself.

When we first met, we were young and hopeful. But as time passed, we both struggled with addiction and hurt each other with our words.

We became the worst versions of ourselves together, but it was hard to let go because we were so used to each other.

I kept thinking about him all the time, until one day, I realized I hadn't thought about him for a whole week. It was a big moment for me.

During those years, I was with someone else who was very different from my ex. I thought being with someone opposite would protect me, but it also kept me from feeling close to anyone.

Healing didn't happen naturally. It took me a long time to realize that we weren't meant to be together again.

I also realized I had problems with addiction. I smoked, drank too much, and used drugs to escape my feelings.

When I got rid of those bad habits, I saw things more clearly. I understood that I wasn't really in love with my ex; I was just addicted to him.

I thought I needed to learn how to love again, but I didn't. Love was always inside me. I just needed to learn to accept myself and others.

Now, I feel love in simple things like watching a sunset or talking to a friend. I don't need someone else to make me feel loved.

Heartbreak taught me the difference between real love and just wanting someone. It's a chance to learn about yourself and grow.

THE DETACHMENT PROTOCOLS

Now that you understand the dynamics of relationships ending and the grieving process, it's time to tackle your broken heart head-on. So, what's the crucial first step toward healing? It's simple—refrain from reaching out. No calls, no texts, no DMs.

After a breakup, the urge to seek comfort is strong. You might instinctively want to reach out to someone who knows and understands you—perhaps your ex. But this dilemma often feels like banging your head against a wall.

Then again, maybe you're doing just fine without your ex. Maybe you've made positive changes, like finally cleaning your car, a pet peeve of theirs. You might even want to show them you're a different person now, someone they'd want to be with. But therein lies the trap: the person you want to talk to the most is the one you must cut off.

Continuing to communicate with your ex prolongs emotional ties and hinders your ability to move forward. Dr. Susan J. Elliott, a grief counselor, notes that many struggle to cease communication post-breakup, despite knowing it's necessary for healing.

In today's digital age, communication is effortless. Yet, this accessibility complicates breakup recovery. The solution? Strengthen your resolve. Take a moment to center yourself and commit to a communication blackout. Ideally, refrain from contacting your ex indefinitely, but at least maintain it for a month or two.

When initiating this period of no communication, consider informing your ex, especially if you're connected on social media. Send a brief message explaining that you need space to process the breakup. Then, remove all traces of your ex from your contacts and social media to reinforce the boundary.

While you can control what your ex sees on social media, keeping tabs on them can be tempting. Change your relationship status to "single" promptly. It may sting initially, but it helps in moving forward.

Remove your ex from all contact lists, digital or written. If you must keep their contact info, store it out of sight or with a trusted friend until you're ready.

Now comes the tough part: facing the void your ex left. Who do you confide in now? What do you do when all you want is to hear their voice? Breaking up is like quitting a drug—you're psychologically addicted to their company. Withdrawal varies, but reaching out to family and friends can ease the process.

Maintain self-care throughout the day. Exercise, eat well, and prioritize rest. Treat yourself to small joys like dining out or indulging in a book. Redirect your urge to contact your ex by reaching out to someone from your support network instead.

Despite your best efforts, the urge to reach out to your ex may still arise. In such moments, consider adopting techniques from behavioral therapy, such as journaling.

Keep a small notebook within easy reach, and whenever the urge strikes, jot down your thoughts and emotions. Reflect on why you feel compelled to maintain contact and ask yourself probing questions:

- What am I hoping to achieve with this conversation?

- What emotions do I want to evoke in myself and my ex?

- How do I envision the outcome of this conversation?

- What triggers led to this urge to contact my ex?

- Am I seeking attention, even if it's negative?

By analyzing your feelings and motivations, you'll gain clarity on why you're drawn to reconnect. Use this insight to develop strategies to resist the urge. For instance, if you notice a pattern like feeling prompted to call after watching cooking shows, brainstorm alternative activities to distract yourself.

Crafting Your Personal Coping Plan

Creating a plan to avoid contacting your ex isn't just about your interests; it's a personal journey that evolves over time.

Begin by reviewing your journal entries detailing moments when you wanted to reach out. From there, brainstorm activities to distract yourself:

- Take a refreshing shower, engaging your mind away from thoughts of your ex.

- Exercise to release pent-up emotions and boost your mood.

- Enjoy a leisurely walk to clear your mind and regain composure.

- Explore your local mall without feeling obligated to make purchases.

- Reconnect with nature at a nearby park, engaging in free activities.

- Pour your heart out in your journal, gaining clarity on your feelings.

- Immerse yourself in a hobby or craft to regain peace of mind.

- Tend to household chores to create a sense of order and accomplishment.

- Tackle homework or productive tasks to divert your focus from your ex.

Once you've compiled a list, select five or six activities to combat the urge to contact your ex. Display the list near your phone or computer for easy access. Whenever the urge arises, engage in the first activity. Repeat this process until the urge subsides.

If you find yourself contacting your ex despite your efforts, revisit your journal and reassess your coping strategies. Modify your list based on what did or didn't work for you. Remember, this plan is tailored to your needs and preferences, so prioritize activities that resonate with you, even if they differ from others' suggestions.

LETTING GO OF THE MYTH OF VALIDATION AND CLOSURE

One common mistake I see many women make is seeking validation and closure from their exes. They hope for apologies, admissions of mistakes, and acknowledgment of the pain caused. While validation is crucial for healing, longing for it can lead to unhealthy behaviors like constant communication or stalking.

Similarly, seeking closure from an ex can be damaging. It's normal to want closure, but often, it's hard to achieve constructively. Many end up feeling abandoned and devastated when their attempts are ignored. However, relying on your ex for closure is unnecessary and detrimental to your well-being.

It's a misconception that validation and closure must come from your ex. In reality, you can find resolution elsewhere—from supportive friends and family, therapy, and self-reflection. Accepting this fact early on will save you much anguish and pave the way for healing.

While you may agree with this intellectually, the urge to seek validation or closure can still be strong. Resist the temptation to reach out and focus on acquiring the tools needed to disengage and move forward.

When it comes to cutting off contact with an ex, it's common to come up with excuses to justify staying in touch. Grief counselor Dr. Susan Elliott has identified seven main reasons why people feel the need to reach out to their exes, with closure being a significant one.

Seeking closure often involves wanting to understand what went wrong in the relationship, hoping that clarity will bring relief from pain and guilt. However, the belief that closure can only be attained through conversation with the ex is misguided.

Engaging in discussions with your ex about what went wrong may initially seem satisfying, but it rarely provides the closure you seek. Their answers may raise more questions or fail to satisfy your need for understanding. Moreover, there's a risk that seeking closure from your ex may lead to further emotional distress if they respond negatively or refuse to engage.

True closure comes from within and involves accepting that some questions may never have satisfactory answers. It's about acknowledging the experience, learning from it, and moving forward without lingering on unresolved issues.

Accepting that life doesn't always provide clear answers is challenging, but it's essential for personal growth and healing. Instead of seeking closure externally, focus on finding peace within yourself and embracing the lessons learned from the relationship.

Letting Go of the Need to Say "One Last Thing"

Feeling the urge to say "one last thing" to your ex is a common sentiment tied closely with the desire for closure. It's understandable, especially if you were the one who was dumped. The idea that a heartfelt declaration or the right words could reignite the relationship is a prevalent trope in love stories, but reality often paints a different picture.

The truth is, relationships don't unravel overnight. Whether it ended abruptly or through a gradual process, changing your ex's mind with just one conversation is unlikely. It would take time and mutual openness, which may not be feasible or healthy. Persisting beyond this point can border on obsession and may lead to greater emotional turmoil.

Wanting to prove your ex wrong about their perception of you is another motivation for wanting to say one last thing. But seeking validation from someone whose opinion is clouded by the breakup is futile. Your worth isn't defined by their judgment, especially during a time of heightened emotions.

Instead of fixating on what your ex thinks, focus on nurturing your self-worth and moving forward. Accept that their opinion doesn't define you, and prioritize your own emotional well-being. Letting go of the need to have the last word can be liberating and mark the beginning of your journey towards healing and self-discovery.

Letting Go of "Getting My Stuff Back" Excuses

Using the excuse of retrieving belongings from your ex after a breakup is often a thinly veiled attempt to see them again or justify contact. While it may seem necessary to reclaim your favorite sweater or other items, it's essential to recognize when this justification is merely a guise.

Ideally, both parties should arrange for the return of belongings shortly after the breakup, minimizing the need for prolonged contact. Waiting too long diminishes the validity of the excuse and may complicate matters legally. After a reasonable timeframe, your ex may legally assume ownership of your belongings, adding another layer of complexity.

To streamline the process, gather all items you wish to return or retrieve and create a list. Contact your ex to arrange a mutual exchange, then refrain from further communication afterward.

Additionally, it's important to let go of the expectation of reclaiming gifts given during the relationship. Once gifted, they become the property of your ex, and attempting to retrieve them may only prolong emotional attachment and hinder the healing process.

Reconsidering the "Let's Be Friends" Excuse After a Breakup

While the notion of remaining friends with your ex might seem like a mature and amicable way to navigate the aftermath of a breakup, it often introduces complexities and challenges that hinder the healing process. The desire to maintain a friendship can be rooted in a variety of motivations, but it's essential to carefully evaluate whether this arrangement is truly beneficial for both parties.

Attempting to transition to a friendship immediately after a breakup can impede the process of emotional closure and hinder individual growth. Exploring the ruins of the relationship and resolving lingering feelings requires time and distance from the former partner. Rushing into a friendship prematurely can perpetuate emotional entanglement and prevent the establishment of a healthy, independent identity as a single individual.

Moreover, the history shared with an ex introduces a minefield of potential triggers and sensitive topics that can undermine attempts at friendship. What might be lighthearted banter with a friend can inadvertently reopen wounds or reignite unresolved conflicts when interacting with an ex. The blurred boundaries between friendship and romantic history can complicate communication and lead to further emotional turmoil.

While maintaining a friendship with an ex is not inherently impossible, it should be approached with caution and only considered after sufficient time has passed for both parties to heal and redefine themselves independently. Reflecting on personal motivations for pursuing a friendship, such as a desire to retain companionship without the responsibilities of a relationship, is crucial for making informed decisions.

If either party feels pressured into maintaining a friendship or harbors doubts about its viability, it's important to assert boundaries and prioritize individual well-being. Friendship should be based on mutual consent and genuine connection, rather than obligation or external pressure. Ultimately, the decision to remain friends with an ex should be guided by introspection, honesty, and a commitment to personal growth and emotional health.

STRATEGIES FOR MAINTAINING ZERO CONTACT AFTER A BREAKUP

When it comes to resisting the temptation to reach out to your ex after a breakup, relying solely on willpower can be challenging. Instead, employing specific strategies can help you gather the strength needed to maintain zero contact. Here are three effective methods:

#1 Beware The White Bear:

Psychologically, the more you try not to think about something, the more it occupies your mind. This phenomenon, known as the "white bear effect," illustrates how attempting to suppress thoughts of your ex can actually intensify them. Rather than berating yourself for thinking about your ex, acknowledge these thoughts without acting on them. Avoiding the urge to contact your ex is akin to resisting the allure of a tempting treat in the fridge—acknowledge the temptation but refrain from indulging.

#2 Admire Someone Else:

Seek inspiration from individuals who embody qualities you admire. Whether it's a celebrity or someone in your life, finding a role model who has overcome challenges similar to yours can provide motivation and strength.

Witnessing their resilience and determination can instill a sense of empowerment within you. Reflect on their accomplishments during moments of weakness, allowing their example to guide you toward healthier choices.

#3 Daily Mini Goals:

Create a structured routine for your days, especially during periods when you have ample free time. Plan achievable tasks and goals to keep yourself occupied and focused on productive activities. These mini goals serve as distractions from thoughts of your ex and provide a sense of accomplishment. Whether it's walking the dog, decluttering a room, or engaging in hobbies, each task keeps your mind occupied and prevents idle moments that may lead to contacting your ex.

Remember to document your progress and reward yourself for each successful day of maintaining zero contact. Celebrate your achievements, no matter how small, as you navigate through the challenges of post-breakup healing. With dedication and perseverance, you will gradually regain control over your emotions and move forward with renewed strength and resilience.

I DESERVE BETTER

Tears fall like rain, heartache like pain

A soul worn thin, a love that's in vain

But in the depths of sorrow, a whisper remains

"I deserve better", a truth that regains

The memories linger, a bittersweet refrain

But don't let them define, the love you obtain

You are worthy of warmth, of gentle care

Of arms that hold tight, and a love that's fair

Your heart beats with hope, your spirit with grace

You deserve the sunshine, after the darkest place

A love that uplifts, that heals and restores

A love that celebrates, the beauty you adore

So hold on to hope, and let go of the pain

Remember "I deserve better", and love will reign

In the depths of your soul, a new dawn will rise

And you'll find the love, that meets your worthy eyes.

CHAPTER 3

PLAYING THE EX GAMES

So far, we've discussed the importance of cleanly moving on from your previous relationship. Nevertheless, unless a significant change occurs, such as one of you relocating to another city, the likelihood is high that you'll cross paths with your ex again. In the best-case scenario, you'll have prior notice of your ex's presence, and the occasion will be sufficiently large to avoid awkward encounters. In the worst-case scenario, you might find yourself sharing a workspace with your ex in a class you dislike, making it challenging to move on.

How should you handle these encounters? What's the appropriate demeanor? And what if your ex is already back in the dating scene? Surprisingly, most relationship advice overlooks this aspect, assuming you'll behave politely but cautiously, as one does with an unwanted acquaintance. The reality, however, is that encountering your ex triggers a whirlwind of thoughts — from deciding on safe conversation topics to navigating potential conflicts and determining your end goal. And then there's the added concern of how to react if your ex tries to provoke you.

Although facing your ex might seem like tiptoeing through a minefield barefoot, it doesn't have to be so daunting. There are strategies you can employ to ease these interactions.

ESTABLISHING BOUNDARIES

I found this journal entry from the beginning of my journey into setting boundaries. In bold black ink, it reads, "I wish I could be honest about my feelings. If I can learn to do that before I die, I'll be content." It might seem dramatic, but I was fed up with always accommodating others and trying to please everyone.

I wrote this the day after experiencing unwanted advances at a bar. A stranger had aggressively engaged me in conversation, mixed with flirtation, and even put his hand on my waist for about thirty minutes. I endured it with a fake smile until I could escape to the bathroom.

As usual, I couldn't bring myself to assert my boundaries. I stayed silent, hoping he would pick up on my discomfort and back off. But he didn't. The next morning, I grabbed my pen and identified my biggest challenge: setting boundaries, being honest about my needs, and listening to my inner self.

This challenge affected every aspect of my life. My constant need to please others created imbalances in my relationships—with friends, partners, and colleagues. Sometimes, it was as simple as enduring a boring conversation for too long or offering help when I had none to spare. Other times, it was as extreme as being intimate with someone I didn't want to be with just to avoid hurting their feelings.

I was betraying myself over and over again, molding my life around the desires of others. It left me feeling unfulfilled and disconnected from my true self.

From a young age, women are taught to prioritize others' needs over their own. But I realized that I had to take responsibility for my own happiness, especially after a tough breakup.

That breakup was a wake-up call—a chance to build a supportive relationship with myself, the woman beneath the people-pleasing facade. For the first time, I committed to prioritizing my own needs, setting clear boundaries, and being honest with others. And that decision changed everything.

If you often wish you'd stood up for yourself in conflicts, feel drained in social situations because you're putting on a performance, overcommit to obligations while neglecting activities that bring you joy, agree to be intimate with people you later regret, or feel like you give more than you receive in relationships, this can be the year to break the pattern and start speaking your truth.

Here are nine tips that simplify the process of setting boundaries into practical habits.

1. Recognize your emotions in your interactions with others.

Identify challenging feelings like overwhelm, anger, or frustration, as they can guide you in understanding when, where, and with whom to set boundaries. These emotions indicate that someone may be encroaching on your personal space or time. Becoming more aware of your own emotions will help you establish meaningful boundaries in the future.

Instead of ignoring your emotions, ask yourself, "What am I feeling? Why do I feel this way? What needs to change for me to feel safer?"

2. Begin with a well-being statement.

Before discussing boundaries, start the conversation with a statement to set a compassionate and open tone. This can be particularly useful when you're worried about disrupting long-established patterns in long-term relationships with family or partners.

Kickstart the conversation by sharing your commitment to setting boundaries. Explain why it's important for your well-being and how it can benefit you. Focusing on your own well-being initiates a meaningful discussion centered on the undeniable value of your health and happiness.

3. Appreciate when others set boundaries.

People who struggle to set boundaries often find it difficult to respond when others set limits. Before I started setting my own boundaries, I used to feel dismissed, angry or rejected when friends or lovers set boundaries. However as I realized that people establish boundaries to protect their well-being, I intentionally developed an attitude of gratitude. I responded to others with phrases like "I value your honesty" or "I appreciate you sharing that with me," even when the boundary was tough to accept. These friends and lovers became role models, showing me what a healthy, well-boundaried life could look like.

4. Learn to say "no thanks" without explaining.

You might feel the need to justify your boundaries to others, but sometimes the simplest and most honest response is "No, thanks." Explaining or making excuses can lead to feelings of guilt or misalignment with your inner self. Practice saying "No, thanks" without elaboration. Start small, like saying "No, thanks" when your housemate suggests watching a TV show or declining a drink at a bar.

5. Create a VIP-Only list.

Without clear boundaries, you may tend to overshare personal information. While honesty is important, sharing too much too quickly can make others uncomfortable and leave you feeling excessively exposed. If you have a history of oversharing, establish a VIP-only list of sensitive topics to discuss only with trusted individuals who make you feel safe and understood. Using this list as a guideline will help you build self-trust, maintain your privacy, and form a circle of reliable confidants.

6. Take a break from a toxic friendship.

Perhaps you have a friend who consistently uses you as a sounding board for their problems or requests favors without reciprocating. If you feel that a friend's personal struggles are negatively affecting your well-being, one form of boundary setting is taking a break from the relationship. Remember that prioritizing your well-being is not selfish or cruel. Healthy friendships are mutual and nourishing, not one-sided and draining.

7. Develop a post-boundary-setting mantra.

If you have a history of people-pleasing, setting boundaries may require you to break old patterns, leading to feelings of guilt, selfishness, or embarrassment after setting a completely valid boundary. Be kind to yourself and understand that it takes time to develop your boundary-setting skills. In the meantime, create a mantra to use after setting difficult boundaries with others. It can be as simple as, "I set boundaries to feel safe" or "Setting boundaries is an act of self-love." Your mantra can serve as a reminder that this journey, though challenging, is in your best interest.

8. Find a cheerleader.

Throughout my journey in setting boundaries, I benefited greatly from sharing my successes with a close friend who supported me at every step. She witnessed my progress and helped me acknowledge my achievements when I was self-critical. Set yourself up for success by designating a trusted friend, family member, or partner to be your boundary cheerleader. Explain your intention to set better boundaries and your desire for a supportive companion throughout the process. When you establish a new boundary, inform your cheerleader, and make time for both of you to celebrate your success, whether in person, over the phone, or with a simple high-five emoji.

9. Envision a transformed life.

Instead of dwelling on reducing oversharing and people-pleasing, imagine the positive changes that will result from setting boundaries. Allow yourself to envision how your life will improve when you start speaking your truth. How will you change? How will your daily life become more fulfilling? How might you experience more authenticity in your relationships? Keep this vision in mind as you make decisions that are in your best interest, day by day.

Boundaries are tools that empower us to feel safe, strong, and in control of our relationships. As your journey continues, you'll begin to understand that it's not only your right but your responsibility to make choices that prioritize your well-being.

OVERCOMING DESTRUCTIVE HABITS

The overwhelming mix of rejection and loss post-breakup can be challenging to articulate adequately. These emotions can send your mental state spiraling and leave you overwhelmed with debilitating anxiety, often leading to the development of harmful habits in an attempt to cope.

The reality is, these habits must be confronted head-on; there's no bypassing the discomfort they bring during a breakup. However, the silver lining lies in recognizing and addressing these habits. Below are some common post-breakup pitfalls to consider:

Bad Habit #1 – Social Isolation

Many find themselves retreating to their beds or couches for days on end, barely moving except for necessary functions. Sleep becomes elusive, plagued by haunting dreams of the breakup. The thought of facing others becomes daunting, compounded by the fear of encountering reminders of happier times with the ex-partner.

I recall a particular instance in a store where a DVD triggered memories of shared laughter with my ex. The surge of nausea was overwhelming, driving me back home, questioning whether normalcy was ever attainable again.

The inclination to avoid social interactions during this period is understandable, yet detrimental in the long run. Taking the challenging first steps toward socialization is crucial for healing. If you're grappling with these feelings, know that seeking support and venturing out is vital.

Seek Support from Existing Friends

Have certain friends attempted to reach out to you, only to be met with resistance? While some may seek gossip or satisfy curiosity, genuine concern exists among others. Imagine yourself in their shoes – wouldn't you want to offer support if the roles were reversed? Though it may feel humiliating to expose your vulnerability, true friends will offer support, not judgment.

Consider Reconnecting with Old Friends

It's common to drift from friends during relationships, especially if they're disapproved of by partners. I've experienced this firsthand, allowing fear of solitude to manipulate my actions, relinquishing control of my social circle.

If this resonates with you, consider reconnecting with old friends. It may be challenging initially, but honesty about past actions can pave the way for renewed connections. While not all friendships may regain their former strength, the possibility of forgiveness and empathy is worth the effort.

While rejection from old friends may sting, view it as a learning experience rather than a defeat. Take steps to mend relationships, but accept that not all paths will lead to reconciliation. Learn, grow, and move forward with the knowledge gained from the experience.

Bad Habit #2: **Vengeful Thoughts**

The allure of revenge is undeniable, even if admitting to such thoughts can be uncomfortable. In the aftermath of a breakup, particularly if betrayal is involved, the desire for retribution can be overpowering.

I'll concede, I've entertained thoughts of revenge myself. It's a natural part of the healing process, though hurtful revenge no longer crosses my mind today. Through the dark phases, we emerge as stronger individuals once the dust settles.

However, revenge doesn't necessarily require active pursuit. Redirecting that energy toward self-improvement—focusing on your well-being, success, and happiness—can serve as its own form of revenge. By prioritizing personal growth, you inadvertently create a version of yourself that surpasses your former self and, in turn, makes your ex pale in comparison.

This bittersweet revenge, stemming from self-love and personal growth, can evoke a range of emotions in your ex—jealousy, envy, or even attempts to reconnect. But by then, your focus is squarely on your own journey, rendering external reactions inconsequential.

Ultimately, the most potent 'revenge' is moving on from your ex and crafting a fulfilling life for yourself, continually evolving as an individual. However, it's important not to make this your sole objective; rather, focus on self-improvement, and the rest will fall into place.

I empathize with the urge to seek revenge as a response to pain and rejection, especially when media often glamorize the notion. But I assure you, revenge isn't a constructive path. Instead, channel that energy into envisioning your future—where you want to be and the steps needed to get there. Reframe restless thoughts of revenge into positive, forward-thinking endeavors. With practice, this shift becomes more natural, leading to a cascade of ideas and actionable plans.

These incremental changes can accumulate, propelling you forward on your journey toward healing and personal growth.

Bad Habit #3: Excessive Drinking

I'll be the first to admit my guilt in this area. Reflecting on the days when alcohol served as my coping mechanism brings back unpleasant memories akin to a hangover. The extent of my consumption, as evidenced by the scattered empty bottles around my kitchen, is a testament to the depth of my struggle.

I often turned to alcohol to numb the pain and alleviate the torment of restless nights plagued by nightmares. Without it, I'd find myself grappling with dreams where my ex and I reconciled, only to awaken to the harsh reality of rejection—an emotional agony like no other.

Using alcohol as a crutch in the aftermath of a breakup is a common but detrimental practice. While occasional indulgence in bouts of emotional release may occur, habitual reliance on alcohol to suppress thoughts and feelings can lead to harmful consequences.

If you sense that alcohol consumption has become excessive, acknowledging the issue is a crucial first step. It's imperative to reclaim control of your emotions, steering away from the self-destructive path of relying on alcohol as a means of coping. Remember, alcohol is a depressant, exacerbating emotional turmoil when misused.

Personally, it took me longer than it should have to recognize the severity of my reliance on alcohol. Despite gentle warnings from friends and family, I persisted, even indulging during work breaks and neglecting responsibilities. Only when other areas of my life began to crumble did I realize action was imperative. Pouring out the contents of my bottles was the initial step toward recovery.

During moments when the urge to seek solace in alcohol arises, consider the broader implications. Using alcohol to suppress emotions merely prolongs the pain of the breakup and increases vulnerability, potentially leading to regrettable attempts to reconnect.

In my journey to recovery, I replaced alcohol with healthier alternatives like juices and water. I focused on redirecting negative impulses and reinforcing positive affirmations during vulnerable moments.

I'm not suggesting complete abstinence from alcohol, but exercising caution during this emotionally taxing period is paramount. If necessary, confide in a trusted friend or family member for support.

Bad Habit #4: Rebound Encounters

During my last breakup, a friend suggested that the quickest way to move on from my ex was to seek solace in the arms of someone new. Initially repelled by the idea, I found myself inundated with distressing images and comments on social media, showcasing my ex's seemingly effortless transition into new relationships. It was in response to this emotional turmoil that I decided to heed my friend's advice and engage in a rebound encounter with someone I met on a dating app.

However, the aftermath of this encounter left me feeling even more despondent. Far from alleviating my heartache, it intensified my longing for the comfort and familiarity of my ex. I realized too late that I had acted impulsively, succumbing to misguided advice that only exacerbated my emotional turmoil.

Intuition, guided by your heart and mind, will indicate when it's appropriate to pursue new connections. Unfortunately, I rushed into it prematurely and with the wrong person. For some, seeking solace in temporary encounters may provide temporary relief, but in reality, it merely postpones the true healing process, allowing unresolved pain to fester beneath the surface.

The allure of seeking refuge in the arms of another after a breakup is understandable. Yet, it's crucial to recognize that such distractions offer fleeting comfort at best, ultimately leaving you feeling devalued in the long run. Instead of seeking temporary fixes, prioritize self-care and personal growth.

Consider whether the 'you' in twelve months' time would look back favorably on impulsive hookups as a viable solution to heartbreak. Chances are slim. Rather than succumbing to toxic distractions, focus on your long-term goals and aspirations.

I discovered that confronting my destructive tendencies was the catalyst for positive change. Redirecting my energy toward self-improvement, I embarked on a journey of personal development. I enrolled in night classes to pursue my psychology degree, asserted myself in the workplace, and meticulously planned my future.

Harnessing the negative emotions that had consumed me, I channeled them into constructive actions. Before long, I found myself reflecting on my progress with pride, realizing that my journey from despair to empowerment had been fueled by resilience and determination.

Bad Habit #5: Idealization

Idealizing a past relationship is akin to locking yourself in an emotional prison, fixating on the idyllic moments shared with your ex while conveniently overlooking the flaws. It's a common trap that many find themselves ensnared in after a breakup, but the key to liberation lies within your grasp.

When we idealize an ex, we paint them in a light of perfection, conveniently glossing over their imperfections and the real reasons behind the breakup. This idealization serves as a shield, shielding us from confronting the painful truth of the relationship's end. However, indulging in these idealistic fantasies only prolongs the grieving process, preventing us from moving forward.

If you find yourself succumbing to prolonged bouts of idealization, it's essential to confront these thoughts head-on. One effective strategy is to document the relationship's timeline, warts and all. Include both the highs and lows, acknowledging your own faults as well as your ex's. This exercise offers a sobering perspective, allowing you to break free from the shackles of idealization.

By confronting the reality of the relationship, you'll experience a range of emotions that will ultimately facilitate your journey toward healing and acceptance. So, instead of clinging to idealistic illusions, dare to face the truth, and liberate yourself from the confines of your emotional prison.

PRESERVING YOUR MENTAL WELL-BEING

Experiencing heartbreak can often consume your thoughts entirely. It's natural to dwell on the breakup and replay every moment of the relationship in your mind, searching for answers. Yet, fixating on the past inhibits progress. To move forward, prioritize your mental and physical health.

Your mental state profoundly impacts your ability to heal. Negativity prolongs the healing process, while a positive mindset facilitates recovery and fosters resilience. Cultivating positivity not only aids in overcoming heartbreak but also equips you to navigate future challenges with ease. Fortunately, several strategies can help maintain mental fitness.

Rebuilding Self-Esteem

First and foremost, a breakup often shatters self-esteem. Whether blaming oneself entirely for the relationship's end or scrutinizing physical flaws in the mirror, the aftermath can inflict deep emotional wounds. Moreover, pervasive societal norms often exacerbate low self-esteem, perpetuating a cycle of self-doubt and criticism.

However, resources exist to bolster self-esteem and foster self-acceptance. Here are practical tips to mend emotional wounds and cultivate self-worth:

1. *Identify Your Strengths:* Everyone possesses strengths, even if they're not immediately apparent. Seek input from friends and family to uncover your unique qualities. Compile a list of at least four or five strengths and keep it in a readily accessible location. Remind yourself of these strengths during moments of self-doubt or insecurity.

2. *Embrace Imperfection:* Recognize that nobody is flawless, including those you admire. Avoid comparing yourself unfavorably to others, as everyone grapples with their own shortcomings. Focus instead on accepting yourself, flaws and all.

3. *Nurture Your Talents:* Channel your energy into activities that showcase your strengths. Whether it's writing, performing, or simply helping others, engage in projects that align with your abilities and interests.

4. *Celebrate Achievements:* Acknowledge and celebrate your successes, no matter how small. Allow yourself to bask in the satisfaction of a job well done, without fear of appearing arrogant.

5. Push Your Boundaries: Challenge yourself to step outside your comfort zone and undertake new experiences. Whether it's learning a new skill or volunteering, surpassing self-imposed limitations fosters self-confidence and personal growth.

6. Surround Yourself with Positivity: Limit exposure to negative influences and seek out supportive relationships. Surrounding yourself with people who appreciate and uplift you fosters a nurturing environment for self-growth and acceptance.

7. Eliminate Negative Thinking Patterns: Once you've minimized external criticism, it's imperative to address internal negativity. Negative self-talk can hinder personal growth and perpetuate a cycle of failure. When negative thoughts arise, interrupt them immediately. Take a brief moment to center yourself, perhaps through deep breathing exercises. Acknowledge your limitations, but counter them with positive affirmations. For instance, if you fear being a subpar partner due to communication struggles, acknowledge this challenge, but also recognize your strengths, such as remembering important dates.

8. Conduct Honest Self-Assessment: After curbing negativity, assess your weaknesses objectively. Rather than succumbing to discouragement, view weaknesses as areas for growth. Develop strategies to overcome these challenges, such as implementing organizational tools to manage responsibilities effectively. Remember, the goal is self-improvement driven by personal fulfillment, not a quest to validate self-worth.

9. Cultivate Self-Appreciation: Recognize and celebrate your daily accomplishments, no matter how small. Whether it's staying organized, mastering a difficult task, or completing mundane chores, acknowledge your efforts and take pride in them. Cultivating a habit of self-appreciation fosters a positive self-image and bolsters self-esteem.

10. Embrace the Journey: Understand that building self-esteem is a gradual process. Set realistic, achievable goals and focus on incremental progress. Instead of fixating on the end goal, concentrate on daily victories. By consistently practicing self-affirmation and highlighting strengths, you'll gradually notice a significant improvement in self-perception and confidence, empowering you to engage more confidently in social interactions and personal endeavors.

LEARNING TO TAKE CARE OF YOURSELF

After a breakup, it's easy to lose sight of who we are and what we deserve. That's where self-care steps in. Self-care means actively choosing behaviors to help balance out the stress caused by the breakup, rather than burying it.

Self-care can be a powerful way to heal and rediscover yourself. Many people find that they become stronger versions of themselves when they practice self-care techniques. I know it was true for me—I was at rock bottom after my breakup, but I managed to turn things around.

I remember telling a friend during that tough time, "I just want to stop feeling this pain." Looking back, I'm amazed by the strength I found in myself during that period of heartache. It's incredible what we're capable of as humans, even in our darkest moments.

With some self-care, learning to be kind to yourself, and following the advice in this book, you'll be on the path to becoming the person you deserve to be. Self-care might sound big and overwhelming, but it's not. Sometimes, it won't feel like you're doing much at all. Some days, it'll be easy, and other days, it'll be tough.

In this section, I'll share some self-care techniques that fall into three categories: mind, body, and soul.

Mind

Taking care of your mind is crucial, especially during tough times like a breakup. Here are some techniques to help recharge your mind:

1. Disconnect for an hour: Turn off your phone, unplug your devices, and let your mind unwind. Listen to the sounds around you and let your thoughts wander.

2. Change your route to work: Shake up your routine by taking a different route to work. It might take longer, but it's a simple way to keep your mind active.

3. Prioritize yourself: Make it a point to do something just for you every day. It could be anything that brings you joy.

4. Declutter: Clear out any physical clutter, whether it's your wardrobe or your workspace. A tidy environment can do wonders for your mental clarity.

5. Step out of your comfort zone: Challenge yourself to do something new, like striking up a conversation with a coworker or attending a meeting.

6. Clean up your social media: Unfollow or mute accounts that bring negativity into your life. Surround yourself with positive influences.

7. People-watch: Spend some time observing the world around you. It can be surprisingly inspiring and refreshing for your mind.

Body

1. Deep Breaths: Take a moment to breathe deeply. Inhale for six seconds, exhale for seven. Repeat this three times. It helps reduce stress, anxiety, and panic by oxygenating your body.

2. Herbal/Green Teas: Enjoy a cup of herbal or green tea. These teas not only flush out toxins but also uplift your mood with their refreshing scents. Pair it with some light reading for a relaxing break.

3. Healthy Eating: Choose two healthy breakfasts, lunches, and dinners for your week. Stick to these choices and aim to drink two liters of water a day. Nourishing your body from the inside out can have a positive impact on your emotional well-being.

4. Treat Your Body: Pamper yourself with a comforting body moisturizer or a new shower wash. Taking care of your body can promote better sleep, which is essential during tough times like a breakup. Treat yourself a little.

5. Exercise: Take a walk or go for a run to release endorphins and improve your physical health. Even if it's just walking laps around your home or climbing stairs, make it a priority for your well-being.

6. Music Therapy: Turn on some upbeat music and let yourself dance. Music can uplift your mood and motivate you to overcome challenges. You can even combine dancing with decluttering for a double dose of self-care.

7. Connect with Nature: Spend time outdoors, soaking up the sun and enjoying the greenery. Whether it's sitting on a park bench or taking a stroll, allow yourself to relax and let your mind wander freely.

Soul

1. Help Others: Even when you're struggling, small acts of kindness can make a big difference. Offer to carry someone's heavy bags or help out a coworker. Being kind, even in small ways, can bring unexpected rewards.

2. Date Yourself: Treat yourself to a solo date night. Light candles, play soothing music, and enjoy a nice meal—

even if it's takeout. Taking care of yourself doesn't have to be complicated.

3. Find Beauty Everywhere: Make it a mission to notice the beauty in everyday things. Whether you're walking home or shopping, look for the small details that make life beautiful. Challenge yourself to find five beautiful things on your next outing.

4. Take a Solo Break: Spend some time alone, away from your usual routine. Explore a nearby town or city, indulge in new experiences, and embrace solitude. It's during moments like these that we truly get to know ourselves better.

5. Don't Be Afraid to Ask for Help: Whether it's at work or in your personal life, reaching out for assistance can be empowering. Everyone needs help sometimes, and admitting it is a positive step toward overcoming challenges.

6. Keep a Thought Diary: Writing down your thoughts and feelings can be a cathartic way to release negativity. Use a journal to reflect on your day, note any highs or lows, and set intentions for tomorrow.

7. Spread Positivity: Engage with others through small gestures like smiling at a stranger or chatting with your

barista. These simple acts can fill your soul with positive energy and brighten your day.

Each step you take towards self-care brings you closer to where you want to be in life. As you nurture yourself, you'll start to feel the fog lifting and a deeper connection to yourself. Create your own self-care routines based on what works best for you—whether it's morning runs, healthy breakfasts, or stepping out of your comfort zone.

By practicing these small actions consistently, you'll develop healthy habits that lead to a brighter future. You'll emerge from heartbreak with a renewed sense of hope, positivity, and happiness.

UNSHACKLED

Chains of habit, forged in pain

Bound me tight, in a cycle of shame

But I've found the strength, to break the chain

And rise up, from the ashes again

The weight of bondage, I no longer bear

Free to move forward, without a care

The shackles of shame, they no longer hold

I'm unshackled, my spirit now unfold

The grip of destruction, it loosens its hold

As I embrace, a new path to mold

A journey of freedom, of hope and of grace

Where love and self-care, take their rightful place

CHAPTER 4

MOVING ON

SELF-SABOTAGE... NO MORE

We often find ourselves criticizing without hesitation, readily putting ourselves down and prioritizing others without feeling guilty. Unaware, we nurture negative thoughts, doubting our worth and abilities in the world. This habit goes unquestioned, leading us to continually sabotage ourselves as a means of self-protection. The belief is that by attacking ourselves first, others won't have the chance to do the same – the damage will already be inflicted by someone familiar: ourselves.

This constant self-sabotage wages an internal war, causing our bodies to endure aggressive and toxic self-talk. It feels unnatural to subject ourselves to such harmful thoughts.

That's why making peace with yourself should be your top priority. Always prioritize self-improvement before anything else. How can you succeed in relationships, career, or life if you haven't first succeeded with yourself?

So, how do you achieve inner peace? How do you begin to love yourself?

1. Developing Self-Awareness in Thoughts

Embarking on the journey to a better life begins with self-awareness, a timeless piece of advice encapsulated in the phrase "Know Thyself."

Do you truly know yourself? Are you conscious of the thoughts that occupy your mind? If not, it's time to sharpen your focus. Shift your attention from external factors like the weather, colleagues, classmates, friends, and family. Direct your focus inward. What thoughts are currently circulating in your mind?

Don't falter; persist in your focus. Elevating your consciousness and concentration can be challenging, but the rewards are well worth the effort.

Now that you're gaining insight into the thoughts shaping your mind, body, and spirit, take proactive steps.

How do you take action when the battleground is within you? Transform the game in your favor. Assume control over yourself—the master of your thoughts, emotions, and feelings. Demonstrate to your autopilot brain who's in charge.

To achieve this, enhance your focusing power. Train your brain to heed your commands. Be warned: it won't surrender easily. You'll face initial struggles. The crucial aspect is that whenever you detect a negative, self-destructive thought about yourself or your surroundings, promptly instruct your brain to switch gears. Update the mental operating system by replacing negative thoughts with positive ones.

Implement this habit consistently every day, and you'll witness remarkable changes within and around you. Increased empathy, openness, and adaptability will become your strengths. You'll radiate positivity. As we let our own light shine, we unconsciously give others permission to do the same."

2. Enhancing Self-Awareness in Body Language

Did you know that a whopping 96% of our communication doesn't involve words? It means most of what we express happens through our body language, which is a powerful form of communication with ourselves and others.

Direct your attention to your body. What is your posture conveying right now? What message do you want your body to send to yourself and those around you? Teach your body to follow your lead. Learn to manage your body language.

Every detail matters. How you position yourself, whether you smile or not – it communicates who you are to yourself and those nearby. When you open your arms and lift your head high, you're not just opening up to others but also to yourself and the universe.

You may often find yourself in low-power postures. Swiftly replace these with high-power postures. Project yourself in the way you aspire to be seen. Consistently ask yourself: How would the person I want to become appear in this moment?

To feel confident and positive, present yourself as a confident and positive individual. If you avoid eye contact and keep your gaze down, people won't take you seriously, revealing discomfort with yourself and others.

Earn respect from others by first respecting yourself. It all begins with what your body language conveys about you. Never underestimate the influence of your body language, your voice tone, your walk, and your gestures. Every aspect communicates something about you, and people will notice.

Become at ease with your body, and it will cooperate, taking you wherever you wish to go. If you desire confidence, compel your body to exude confidence.

3. Quality Time Alone

Understanding yourself requires a straightforward step: spend time alone. When getting to know a stranger, we willingly invest hours discussing their interests, who they are, and their positive qualities. Why not extend the same courtesy to ourselves?

It's intriguing how we often prioritize others over ourselves, believing they deserve our time more than we do. Isn't that surprising?

Allocate at least 30 minutes each day exclusively for you. No one else. No external distractions. Wherever you are, whoever you're with, ensure you maintain a strong, meaningful connection with your inner self. Nothing and no one should hinder that connection.

The closest person to you should always be yourself; otherwise, you empower someone outside of you to influence your feelings, actions, and experiences.

Critics may label you as selfish or egoistic, but often, they're projecting their own unhappiness. To grasp the significance of being close to yourself, reach a higher level of consciousness.

You cannot truly thrive or assist others without first helping yourself. To share love with others, you must first give love to yourself. This, in my perspective, is an unwavering principle.

WHAT TO AVOID WHEN STARTING AFRESH

Moving on from a devastating breakup to finding happiness and love again is a journey worth celebrating. Reflecting on my own experiences, I've realized how crucial it is to navigate this transition with honesty and openness. Here are some insights I'd like to share to help you avoid the pitfalls I encountered when starting a new relationship after a breakup:

Tip #1 – Be Honest

It's important to be truthful about your past experiences, especially the pain and emotional scars left by your previous relationship. While you don't need to divulge every detail on the first date, being upfront about your emotional baggage can foster understanding and empathy from your potential partner.

Being vulnerable might feel daunting, but starting a new relationship with honesty lays a strong foundation for trust and authenticity. Pretending to be unaffected or adopting a nonchalant attitude can backfire, leading to misunderstandings and hurt feelings.

In my own journey, I regret not being more open with my current partner about my emotional struggles. My facade of indifference ultimately caused unnecessary pain and prolonged the healing process for both of us. Looking back, I wish I had been brave enough to share my truth from the beginning, saving us both from months of unnecessary turmoil.

Tip #2 – Be Yourself

Embrace your quirks and idiosyncrasies, as they make you unique and interesting. Suppressing your true self to fit a certain mold will only lead to dissatisfaction and misunderstanding in the long run. Remember, authenticity is attractive. My journey taught me that staying true to myself allowed my partner and me to connect on a deeper level, discovering shared quirks and humor along the way.

Tip #3 – Be Adventurous

Stepping out of your comfort zone with your partner can create memorable experiences and strengthen your bond. Embrace new activities and challenges together, whether it's trying a new hobby, exploring a new destination, or attending events. Embracing adventure fosters excitement and growth within the relationship, keeping things fresh and invigorating.

Tip #4 – Be Open

While it's natural to feel guarded after experiencing past hurts, maintaining emotional openness is vital for building trust and intimacy in a new relationship. Communicate openly with your partner about your fears and insecurities, allowing them to understand your emotional landscape. Being vulnerable requires courage, but it paves the way for deeper connections and emotional growth.

Tip #5 – Have Fun

Prioritize your own happiness and fulfillment outside of the relationship. Engage in activities that bring you joy and fulfillment, whether it's pursuing hobbies, spending time with friends, or focusing on personal growth. Cultivating a fulfilling life outside of the relationship not only enhances your overall well-being but also makes you more attractive and desirable to your partner.

Tip #6 – Be Mindful

Pay attention to your instincts and intuition when navigating a new relationship. Be mindful of any red flags or warning signs that may arise, and don't ignore them out of fear of being alone or starting over. Trust your gut feelings and maintain emotional integrity, as it will ultimately lead to healthier and more fulfilling relationships in the long run.

By embracing these tips and remaining true to yourself, you'll navigate the complexities of new relationships with confidence, authenticity, and resilience. Remember, every experience, whether positive or negative, contributes to your growth and evolution as a person. Trust in your journey and believe in your ability to overcome challenges and find happiness.

CONCLUSION

I've equipped you with the mental tools I utilized to navigate through my own heartache, and I've opened up about my experiences with the hope that you'll draw inspiration from them, or perhaps find some resonance. Additionally, I penned this book with the intention of extending comfort, reassuring you that you're not traversing this challenging period alone, and assuring you that this difficult phase will eventually fade. My aim was to provide insight into the steps you can take to move beyond this breakup and onto more promising endeavors.

I extend my heartfelt wishes for your well-being, prosperity, and joy. I firmly believe that these are attainable goals if you persevere through the trials of this time. If there are any aspects I've overlooked or if you have feedback to share about this book, please feel free to leave a review and rating on Amazon. If you're inclined, consider sharing a brief account of your own breakup journey in your review, offering hope to others in similar situations. Your thoughts on how this book has aided you, whether as a source of guidance, solace, or both, would be greatly valued.

Here's to overcoming your breakup and embarking on brighter paths. I have every confidence that you're capable of achieving it.

I AM GOING TO HEAL

In the depths of my soul, a spark remains

A glimmer of hope, through the tears and the pain

I am broken, but I am not undone

I am wounded, but I will be made whole again

The darkness may whisper, "You'll never be free"

But I know the truth, that I am meant to be

A survivor, a warrior, a heart that's strong

I will rise up, and I will move forward, all day long

With every step, with every breath I take

I am going to heal, I am going to make

A new path, a new story, a new me

Free from the chains, of what used to be

Made in the USA
Las Vegas, NV
08 January 2025